THE
Archive Photographs
SERIES

GRIMSBY

An aerial view of the Fish Dock, showing Ross House and trawlers tied up. On the bottom right is the slipway for repairing vessels.

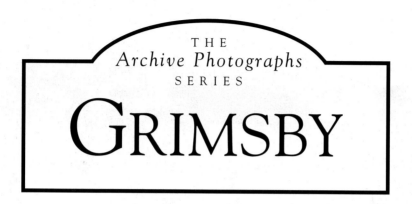

THE
Archive Photographs
SERIES

GRIMSBY

Compiled by
David and Pearl Armstrong

CHALFORD

First published 1997
Copyright © David and Pearl Armstrong, 1997

The Chalford Publishing Company
St Mary's Mill, Chalford,
Stroud, Gloucestershire, GL6 8NX

ISBN 0 7524 1067 9

Typesetting and origination by
The Chalford Publishing Company
Printed in Great Britain by
Bailey Print, Dursley, Gloucestershire

One of the wooden sailing smacks.

Contents

Acknowledgements

We are very grateful to The Grimsby Museum Service for allowing us to use the photographs and to their staff, especially Chris Volley, for their valuable assistance. We would also like to thank Mrs McCarthy for the loan of the Tickler electioneering photograph and the many other people who have donated photographs to the Museum Service. In case of any errors, we apologise in advance.

David and Pearl Armstrong
August 1997

Introduction

Life in a community is constantly changing, just as many old buildings have had to make way for modern ones, and it is really interesting to look back and see some things which we remember ourselves. Quite lengthy discussions can follow a slide show in which the march of time has been shown. The authors are not local historians, though they have learned a lot while selecting the photographs. Even street names provide a clue to what has gone before, and many people never realised it.

It can be seen from some of the earlier photographs that there was once a very rural atmosphere in the town and surrounding area until the arrival of the railway, which unfortunately cut the town of Grimsby in two. Its geographical situation meant that communications were, and are still, not ideal, and the railway brought mixed blessings. The docks were under development and rail distribution for the fish and cargoes from the docks was valuable, but as road traffic increased, so did congestion at the level crossings. This often occurred at Cleethorpe Road, renowned for the number of times that the gates were closed, until eventually a flyover was built, but shortly afterwards road distribution started to grow.

The familiar landmark of Grimsby is the hydraulic Dock Tower, dating from 1852 and built with one million bricks, measuring over 300 feet high. It was recently attractively floodlit. The fishing industry attracted families here from other places and the town was also a reception centre for emigrants from the Continent in particular. The Royal Dock Station, built in 1848, was converted so that as many as 300 people could sleep there for one night before moving on, often to Liverpool and the United States. In 1861 the population had reached 11,000, quite an increase in twenty years, and by 1871 was nearer to 40,000. Conditions in the town seem to have been very poor until this time, but were steadily improving at about the time that photography was used to record the development of the railway and docklands areas. Many photographers did not venture far in those days and fortunately turned their cameras to what was happening every day around them. Studio portraits also gained in popularity, though many do not have names or dates on the reverse, something useful for future historians.

The docks have always been a magnet for photographers, and there are many excellent pictures which have been taken over the years. The attractive wooden sailing smacks, followed by iron-built steam trawlers in the early 1880s, make nostalgic images now, but the men going out to sea suffered severe hardships in hazardous conditions. For instance, in 1883, 360 men and boys lost their lives in the North Sea. Ice would be brought in on Norwegian barques to help keep the fish fresh before ice factories were built in the town and later the technique of freezing fish and other foods was an enormous improvement.

The early forms of road transport have been well recorded in the town. Horse-drawn trams were in use up to the turn of the century, followed by steam and electric trams, then trolley buses, until in 1927 petrol buses were appearing on the streets. There were also some strange types of personal transport. The streets were not so busy in those days, and the town would turn out in force for special occasions, such as royal visits and parades, which were captured on plate or film. Hobbies and sports have also been recorded and the town became well provided with places of entertainment and relaxation.

At the time of the First World War the Yarborough and Heneage families were the two main land owners, a large number of streets sprang up with connected names and the town grew apace. The town did not escape the effects of war, as ports were often a target for the enemy.

In 1949 a development plan for Grimsby schools was approved and new schools were built, mostly in the 1950s and 1960s to replace some, but not all, of the old buildings. Another major step, not entirely successful it is felt nowadays, was the building of the high rise flats near Freeman Street in the late 1960s.

The latest change in local administration is that Grimsby and neighbouring Cleethorpes became the unitary authority of North East Lincolnshire in 1996. The majority of the photographs in this edition are from the many stored by the Grimsby Museum Service in the Welholme Museum Store (formerly Welholme Galleries).

The authors came across pictures taken by former members of the Grimsby Photographic Society, which celebrated its centenary in 1994. They are the present secretaries and found it gratifying to see albums of photographs taken by Arthur Stephenson. Bill Hallgarth was also a member of the society, but not many knew that he was gathering together what is now the Hallgarth Collection, quite unique in its size and variety. A few of the authors' own photographs taken in the 1950s and 1960s have been included. They found it a delight to make the choice of pictures for this version of Grimsby in old photographs and hope that many people connected with the town will also derive pleasure from seeing this new collection. It is hoped, too, that present-day situations are going to be as well recorded for posterity.

This introduction is only a brief mention of the period covered by the selection of photographs, but many of these earlier photographers would be quite amazed by the progress made since then in cameras, films and techniques, as we now enter the digital age.

One
Street Scenes

Victoria Street in the early 1930s.

The Oddfellows' lifeboat outside the Corn Exchange on 17 August 1868.

The Catholic procession passing Sir George and Lady Doughty, 1910.

Victoria Street looking east, *c.* 1875. This is one of the main shopping streets.

Looking up Victoria Street, *c.* 1908. The head post office, centre left, has now moved to the old Lees building, and the post office has been converted into an Argos superstore. Musgrave's shop was on the corner of George Street.

The Foundation Ceremony at Moss Road Power Station.

The old bandstand in People's Park, c. 1910.

Hope Street decorated for the Coronation of George V, 22 June 1911. The street was one of the poorest in the town but was always well decorated for special events.

St Mary's Church May Day procession in Heneage Road, 1915.

Wellowgate, showing Hodgson's and Dixon's shops. F. Grange, the small boy aged nine, later owned Mayfield Dairies sometime around 1920.

Brighowgate, *c.* 1920.

'The Siamese Twins' getting ready for one of the 'biggest ever' parades, *c.* 1932.

A general view of People's Park, opened in 1883 by the Duke and Duchess of Connaught.

The tank in People's Park, 1920s.

Corporation Bridge over Alexandra Dock, 7 August 1940.

The Queen and the Duke of Edinburgh visited the Docks and appeared on the balcony of the Town Hall, 28 June 1958.

Nuns Farm, Nuns Corner, a very rural scene, from a Skelton water colour.

Nuns Corner, taken from the college, 1968. It is now one of the busiest junctions in Grimsby.

18

Two
Buildings

The abbey was built on the site of the old Wellow Abbey (dissolved 1536) and was the home of the Wintringham family, 1908.

An engraving of the Collegiate School, Brighowgate, c. 1820.

The Ropery and Ropery Houses, 1847.

The Ropery and Ropery houses at Riby Square, used for a time by the Catholics, 1847.

Weelsby Road Manor House, *c.* 1860.

The Royal Hotel and the Cleethorpe Road level crossing, sometime between 1880 and 1900. It is still very quiet before the traffic started to build up.

Walter Browne's School, Bargate, late Miss Erskine's Nursing Institution and now St James's School, 1862.

Springfield House and Spring Villa, Bargate, with Mr and Mrs Edward Bannister in the foreground, 1870.

The clock tower in the Central Market was donated to the town by Edward Bannister when he was mayor in 1870.

The Newmarket Hotel, *c.* 1900. New Market was later known as Central Market.

GRIMSBY & DISTRICT HOSPITAL.

An engraving of the old hospital in South Parade, which opened in 1877, seen here sometime around 1890.

The Haven flour mill, 1892.

The Victoria schools, later moved to another site nearby.

An engraving of the Corn Exchange, Old Market Place, built in 1857, shown as it was in 1862.

The Corn Exchange, enlarged to show more detail of the building, which replaced the old town hall and other old buildings, *c.* 1900. There had been two other town halls in this area.

The Artillery Volunteer Barracks, opened in 1891, was the headquarters of the First Lincolnshire Royal Garrison Artillery Volunteers. The attractive building on Victoria Street has housed Albert Gait's printing firm for a long time.

The present town hall in Town Hall Square, 1892. The charter was granted in 1201.

Grimsby Town Station, 1892. Behind is the Yarborough Hotel, built in 1851. In recent times it has had a chequered existence, but is now newly refurbished.

People's Park Lodge at the entrance to the park near Ainslie Street.

Welholme Congregational Church, 1906. The building became Welholme Galleries and now Welholme Museum store, where most of the photographs in this book are kept.

The Public Library, Victoria Street, was bombed in the Second World War. The building on the left was the Public Health Office.

St Andrew's Church, Freeman Street, always a landmark when looking from the Hainton Square end, was built on the site of an old mission church.

Details of the interior of St Andrew's Church.

The Red Lion, Nelson Street, in the same area as the above church. There have always been many pubs in the town.

Wintringham Higher Grade School, Eleanor Street, opened in 1895 by Mr Wintringham of The Abbey. It later changed its name to the well-known Wintringham Grammar School. New single sex schools off Weelsby Avenue replaced this building, which still continued to be used by several other educational establishments.

The flats near Freeman Street were built in the late 1960s, when 'high rise' became popular.

Three
Trade and Industry

A group of twenty workmen at an engineering works by Corporation Bridge where MFI is now, c. 1890.

Grimsby Coffee Houses

No. 1 House, "THE CENTRAL,"

Central Market Place.

Every Accommodation for Visitors, Cyclists, and Commercial Travellers.

First=Class Beds,

SEPARATE ROOMS 1/- and 1/6 PER NIGHT.

Tea, Coffee and Cocoa, 1d. per cup, always ready.

DINNERS

EVERY DAY AT TWELVE O'CLOCK.

Roast Beef and Vegetables	...	...	...	6d. & 8d.	per plate.
Roast Mutton and Vegetables	...	...	...	6d. & 8d.	,,
Beef Steak Pudding and Potatoes	...	...	...	4d.	,,
Beef Steak Pie and Potatoes	...	...	...	4d.	,,
Rice Pudding, College Pudding, Jam Roll, or Fruit Tart				2d.	,,

Delicious Chocolate, fresh made, 2d. per cup.

TEA or COFFEE IN SEPARATE POTS, ONE CUP, 2d.
TWO CUPS, 3d.

HAM and EGGS. CHOPS and STEAKS.

HOT WATER FOR TEA.

COMFORT, CLEANLINESS AND MODERATE CHARGES.

No. 2 House—8 FREEMAN STREET, Near Cleethorpe Road.

No. 3 House—29 CLEETHORPE ROAD, Near Dock Station and Royal Hotel.

No. 4 House—120 VICTORIA STREET, Near Town Hall Street.

No. 5 House—3 CLEETHORPE ROAD, NEW CLEE.

Only one minute's walk from the Sands Bridge.

Central Market Place. A leaflet from the Grimsby Coffee Houses advertising their menus.

The *Quenast* unloading at the Riverhead, *c.* 1900.

Cook's butchers shop opposite St James's Church. Mrs Cook is in the doorway and John Allenby on the left, *c.* 1900.

'The monkey, pig and pie shop', close to where Kitchen's surgical shop used to be, near Pasture Street and Victoria Street corner. Apparently, so the story goes, a sailor visited the shop, shouting 'they're after me - look after my monkey!'. The pig and pie were already signs for a pork butcher. The actual statues were taken to Welholme Galleries, and their original site can still be seen.

Opposite: C. & C. Wright, iron and steel merchants, c. 1920. Pictured in the photograph are Joe, ? Ogden and George Ellerby.

Railway Place, Kent Street, opposite Dock Station. Loading lemonade in crates at Gibson's Commercial Hotel.

J. S. Bullen, photographer's shop, No.183 Freeman Street, *c.* 1900. There were several shops of this type in the late 1890s, and samples of their work appear in the 'People' section.

Opposite: Dabb's butchers shop, No. 78 Victoria Street, *c.* 1905. The outside display of wares at butchers' shops seem to have attracted photographers' attention. They would now attract the attention of Environmental Health Officers!

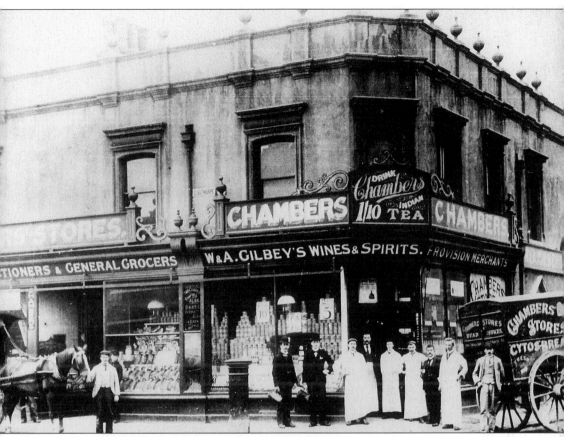

Chambers Stores, Cleethorpe Road, with their own transport, *c.* 1905.

F. L. Marris, chemist, at No. 17 Corporation Road, c. 1905. Mr Marris displays a strange sideline, and one wonders what methods were used for this!

A group of Sleight's workers; the date is unknown.

W. Mudd & Sons, wholesale fish merchants, with very interesting shop front detail.

Dixon's Paper Mill, West Marsh in the 1920s. The aerial view emphasises the extent of the site.

Working at Dixon's Paper Mill.

The entrance to the Grimsby Zoo, *c.* 1910. There will be many Grimbarians who have never heard mention of the zoo.

The flamingoes are proof that there was something beyond the entrance!

Harper Phillips Ltd, Eastgate, carried out work on metal castings. Here a propeller is under construction.

This girl is braiding for the Coal, Salt and Tanning Co. at the time of the heyday of the fishing industry, 1953. Nets and gear were exported by this firm which started sometime around 1890.

The frontage of the Humber Ships' Stores Supply Co. Ltd. The fishing industry provided work for ancillary industries.

The interior of the telephone exchange. There was a large staff, always busy, until automation came in and the staff dwindled every year. Later it became involved with international work, but that too has changed recently.

Opposite: Doig's foundry workers, Humber Street, in the late 1940s or early '50s.

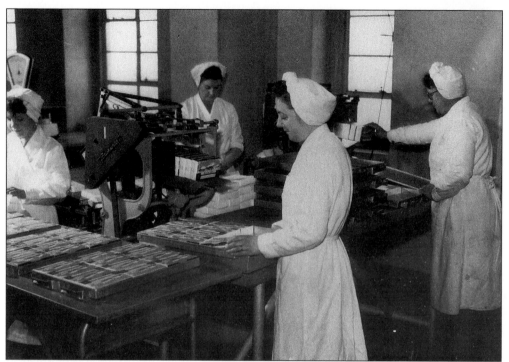

The Ross Group, 1956. Fish processing gradually became more automated, especially when freezing was adopted.

Instead of mostly coal and timber, the Royal Dock vessels were transporting cars by 1962. This has now expanded greatly with modern purpose-built ships regularly coming into Grimsby, rows of new cars can be seen lined up as one leaves the town on the A180 road.

Four

The Docks

An aerial view of the Royal Dock on the left and on the right the Fish Dock, 1961. In the centre is the railway line branching right to Cleethorpes.

Captain John Burns, of the sailing smack *Emma* and one of the first smack skippers. He was presented with a pair of binoculars by the King of Denmark for saving the crew of the Danish vessel *The Ida* on Christmas Day 1871. The photograph was taken by Lowthian Bros in 1880.

LORD NELSON
GRIMSBY COD SMACK
1885

The cod smack *Lord Nelson*, 1885

The Dock Tower and sailing ships in the Royal Dock, c. 1890. Three smaller hydraulic towers were also built for opening the lock gates.

A sailing smack, recorded here as steam starts to be used.

The Royal Dock, either in the late nineteenth or early twentieth century.

Sailing ships in the Royal Dock, *c.* 1920.

Loading carts with fish on the dockside, *c.* 1905.

The Scottish herring lassies gutted and packed the herrings in brine, working in harsh conditions, *c.* 1910

Coal workers by the coal drop, Royal Dock, *c.* 1920.

The steam trawler *Nellie Bruce* GY494, *c.* 1905.

Time for a smoke for the crew of the SS *Ullswater*

The steam trawler *The Northern Duke* GY442.

Steam trawlers, including *Everingham* GY687 and *Glen Kidston* GY227, near the coal hoists, c. 1960.

A shark caught by the *SS Premier, c.* 1898.

The Pontoon, where the fish merchants gathered for the sales in the early morning, early in the twentieth century. It was recently demolished to make way for modern improvements.

Two tugs bringing in a large four-masted sailing ship, c. 1930.

The Fish Dock, well filled.

HMS Grimsby, sloop of the Royal Navy, leaving the Royal Dock, *c.* 1935.

The Grimsby Ice Co. Ltd, *c.* 1930. Operations first began in 1863 to import ice to preserve the fish.

The crew of the *Athelstan* in the 1930s.

Alfred Hartley, one of the crew, on the *Athelstan* in the 1930s.

The trawler *Bedfordshire*, ex-GY196 was converted to a mine sweeper, and lost in 1942.

Mr Keir and Skipper Godfrey of the *St Andrews*.

A crew member takes a solar reading to find the ship's position before the availability of sophisticated navigational equipment.

An unusual scene when the *Ross Kelly* GY6 was being lengthened.

An Icelandic fishing protection vessel, at the time of the 'Cod War', one of the factors in the decline of the fishing industry in Grimsby.

Men on a trawler checking and preparing the fishing gear, c. 1959.

A trawler crew at 'eating stations' enjoying a well-earned rest.

The stoke hold of the *Valafell*, said to be heavy on coal.

Work being carried out on a chimney at the ice company.

Ice blocks on a conveyor at the ice factory in the 1950s. Ice replaced floating wooden chests in the dock used to keep fish fresh.

The watch off duty en route to the Arctic fishing grounds, *c*. 1960.

Icing on a trawler, one of the many hazards for trawlermen.

The deckie-learner takes a crafty nap.

The wireless room of a modern trawler.

Fifteen members of the crew on the deck of the trawler *Hawkins* GY93.

Hauling in the trawl by hand.

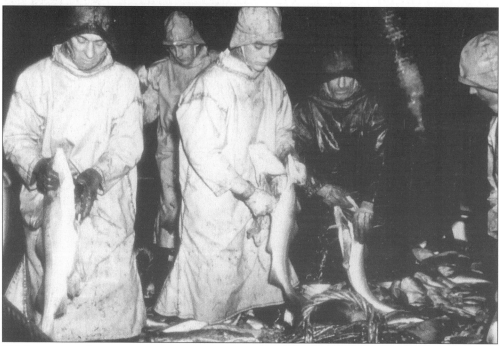

Fish being gutted.

Doig's Yard after the storm on 31 January 1953, when the East Coast suffered severe damage, flooding and loss of life.

A large group of salesmen and buyers, 1955.

Inshore fishing vessels including *Olive* GY59, *Perseverance* H126, *Susan* GY146, *Unity* GY1354, GY72, GY371, GY179 and GY54. Lobster pots are piled high on the jetties, 1962

The stern trawler *Conqueror* GY1364, *c*. 1960.

The *Boston Beverley* stern trawler GY191 in the 1970s.

Shooting the net on a stern-fishing trawler.

Fish merchants at a fish auction, *c.* 1960.

A seine netter at the Pontoon.

The view from the top of Ross House, headquarters of Ross Group, looking down on the Fish Dock, 1968. The future of fishing? On 2 August 1997 the *Jubilee Quest* GY900 complete with all mod cons was launched, at a cost of £1 million, the first new trawler in Grimsby for ten years.

Five

People

A family group photograph from the early years of the century.

Mr Kyme, sail maker, who moved from Salcombe to Grimsby with his family in the mid-1850s.

John Bennington, town crier, c. 1870.

A group of Grimsby's less well-off, photographed in the street around the turn of the century.

Catholic school children in the 1890s.

Nurse Grantham, aged sixty, lived in the Bull Ring and later in No. 5 New Bridge Terrace, *c.* 1890.

The family of Watkinson brothers, known by their initials, were clay pipe makers, who became civic and church leaders in the town. Clay pipes were often provided in the pubs, but eventually briar pipes replaced them because they were stronger.

The Fishermen Songster Brigade, looking prepared for anything.

A portrait taken in the Lowthian
Brothers Studio in Freeman Street,
c. 1896.

Child portraits produced in the Noble
Studio, *c.* 1896.

A group of children posing for
W. Audas, photographer, of No.42
Freeman Street, c. 1896.

The photographer's name of Jancowski
appears on several surviving
photographs, but sadly there are no
details of the models, c. 1896.

This child had a portrait taken by The Eustace Photographic Co., Clee Park Studio, No. 306 Cleethorpe Road, c. 1896.

A portrait taken at the studio of J.W. Walker, of No.152 Cleethorpe Road.

Jenkins and Remy took this lady's portrait, *c.* 1885.

A portrait of Tom Sleight, who lived at No. 194 Heneage Road, taken by Lowthian Brothers, of No.144 and 146 Freeman Street.

An interesting study of a local cobbler, but unfortunately no details are available.

A local sweep in a studio pose.

A class at Hamilton Infants' School, c. 1897.

Miss Sarby with her class at Canon Ainslie School, 1903.

A school photograph, with Timothy Higgins (second row from the back, second on the right), who, at the age of fourteen, saved a man's life in Grimsby Dock.

A group taken outside the tram sheds, Victoria Street, *c.* 1900.

Two of Clover Dairies staff, c. 1920. Clover Dairies were in Victoria Street for many years.

A French onion seller from Brittany calling on Mrs Wilson, Arlington Street, who must have been ready with her camera! The onion sellers were a familiar sight in Grimsby streets.

Frederick Rushworth, one of the trawler owners, c. 1890.

One of Rushworth's fishing apprentices who lived at Albert Terrace, sometime between 1870 and 80. The dog went to sea and was well-known for jumping overboard and recovering fish from the incoming net. Many boy apprentices were from institutions and were very young when taken on.

Sir George Doughty, MP JP, undefeated as MP until 1910, having been elected first as a Liberal in 1895. He rose from a poor beginning to be a leading trawler owner, was mayor from 1892 to 1893 and was knighted in 1904.

T.G. Tickler, on the right of the lower flag, seen electioneering.

Thomas George Tickler was a businessman, famous for his jam factory in Pasture Street. He served the town as MP from 1914 to 1922.

Sir Walter Womersley was the town's MP from 1924 to 1945, when Labour won the seat.

George Skelton, artist and photographer, as a young man. The Skelton collection, in the care of Grimsby Museum Service, contains some beautiful drawings of Grimsby buildings in the days before photography.

W.E.R. Hallgarth. Bill was made an Honorary Member of the Grimsby Photographic Society in 1970. He preserved and collected negatives, photographs and equipment. Some items were rescued by dustmen and given to him! The collection was donated to Welholme Galleries in 1979.

Dame Madge Kendal on the steps of Grimsby Hospital after taking tea. A ward was named after her. With her are Lord Yarborough, T.W. Baskcomb, Matron Brewer, Miss Jackson, Mr L.G. Turpin (hospital secretary) and Mr W.H. Jackson

The entire staff of Lloyds Cars, Patrick Street, 1943.

Dutch children, but no other details are given for the circumstances of this unusual event.

Dutch children, visiting after liberation, at Grimsby Town Station, 1946.

Form 5 Arts A, Wintringham Grammar School, in 1946. The back row includes: Barbara Goring, ? Avril Birkett, Avril Smith, Marion Lister, Joan Eaton, Jean Willmer, Iris Walker, June Stafford, Beatrice Seeley. The centre row includes: Enid Miller, Shirley Bates, Iris Westby, Joyce Dickinson, Valerie Keyworth, Charles Abrahams, Margaret Hobbs, Shirley Haines, Barbara Allen. The front row includes: Victor Small, Mary Charlton, Norman Phillips, Sheila King, Mrs Heyworth, John Dale, Peter Digby, Shirley Robinson, Harold Hugill. Pearl Burman is missing from the photograph as she was on interview. This group entered the school in 1941, spending two years at 'Highfield', a farm with a house and several wooden huts heated by coke stoves. In their third year they moved to the building in Eleanor Street. As it was wartime, there were not many men on the staff. Former pupils were known as 'Old Winghams'. Dr J.H. Walter was headmaster.

The Technical Secondary School had three streams. The girls in the Commercial Stream were learning to type, *c.* 1965.

The staff of the Technical Secondary School, *c.* 1965. Wintringham had by then moved to new buildings, and the 'Tech' occupied their old building. The Whitgift School, opened in 1971, was planned to replace the Technical Secondary School; the headmaster was Mr W.G. Baines after Mr W. Ing.

Six

Transport

Female bus workers in the days when buses had conductors and conductresses.

Delivering milk by the old method of using milk churns and well before milk bottles and cardboard cartons.

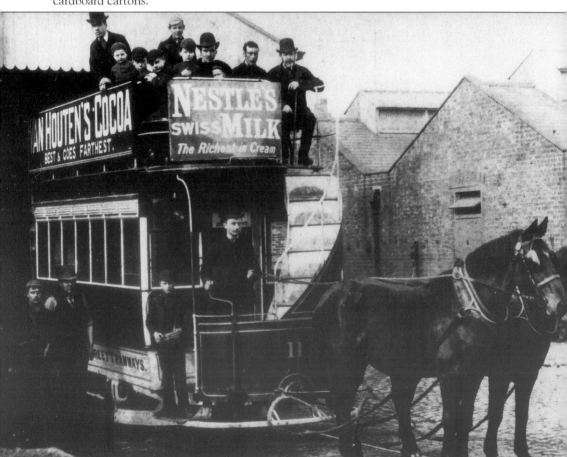

A horse-drawn tram advertising Nestles Milk, c. 1895.

A Dennis 1906, new to Mail Motor and looking rather draughty.

A double decker tram, on its way to the park, *c.* 1930.

A tram rumbles along.

A motor bus, EE313, with an open top and outside stair, c. 1910.

The Yorkshire Engine Company's steam bus in the Old Market Place, 1918.

An open top, double-decker motor bus, EE705, chain driven and with solid tyres, *c.* 1920.

The *Daily Mail* aeroplane was on an advertising tour and landed near Love Lane Corner, 1912.

A Guy eighteen seat runabout, ex-Provincial, 1936.

An open top, double-decker, electric tram, decorated for some special occasion, probably Coronation celebrations, in Cleethorpe Road, 1910.

Another Guy eighteen seat runabout, ex-Provincial, 1936.

A model FE718 with some fashionable attendants, *c.* 1900.

A parade of cars, possibly for a funeral, in Ainslie Street, heading towards People's Park, in the early twentieth century.

A Grimsby and Cleethorpes bus, model EE706.

Charabancs were popular for outings, c. 1910.

The Daimler Kingsway Charabanc BE8305 is shown here in Grafton Street, preparing for an outing.

A motor tricycle with a passenger seat projecting in front and the driver riding over the rear wheel, *c.* 1910.

A three wheel motor bike with a passenger trailer.

Minerva three horse power motor bike FE402, *c.* 1900.

A motor bike with basket-style sidecar seat.

A De Dion twelve spoke FE24, *c.* 1905.

G.W. Pennell riding proudly in his Swiss Martini five seater car, model FE1, *c.*1904.

The Immingham trams had a terminus on Corporation Road. Many workers used them regularly to travel between Grimsby and Immingham.

The last day of the Immingham tram service, 1 July 1961.

Seven
Wartime

Bomb damage in Thesiger Street, 1942. Anderson shelters saved many lives and often remained standing when other buildings were reduced to rubble. One of the authors survived a bomb in a similar shelter in Claremont Road on 27 July 1942.

A group of 'Grimsby Chums', 1915. The Tenth Battalion of the Lincolnshire Regiment was in the Battle of the Somme on the first day with disastrous results. Many were killed or injured.

The Shell Factory workers in Victoria Street in the First World War, *c.* 1918.

Air raid damage in Heneage Road, 1942.

Hope Street, the scene of celebrations in 1911 (page 13), was not spared either in 1942.

South Parade School, not far from the old hospital, was another victim of bombing in 1942, though the heaviest raids were in the following year, and included the unique 'butterfly' anti-personnel bombs.

The Civil Defence Wardens' Service, headquarters staff and Divisional Head Wardens, sometime between 1939 and 1945.

A group of anonymous officers and ratings! If you recognise yourself, please let us know.

Grimsby ARP fire tender crew, sometime between 1939 and 1945.

Captured Italian prisoners of war aboard the requisitioned ex-Grimsby trawler skippered by
Arthur Whittleton, c. 1943.

Members of the WVS and sailors with vegetables, at the Royal Dock, sometime between 1939
and 1945. Rationing did not end until 1954.

Eight

Sport and Entertainment

A stop for a photograph of members of a cycling club wearing uniforms. Cycling was very popular, even the Grimsby Photographic Society had a cycling section in its early days.

Harry Thomas, a keen cyclist and member of Grimsby Cyclists' Club, owned the first Ordinary ('penny farthing') in the town. It was sold in 1879.

Grimsby Ladies' Football Club, 1895. A chance to escape from everyday Victorian clothing.

The Salvation Army band inside the Citadel, in the late nineteenth century.

121

The Prince of Wales Theatre in Freeman Street, *c.* 1907. This picture shows it with the canopy at the front.

Grimsby Town Football Club, a second division promotion team, in the 1928-29 season.

Wintringham Grammar School cricket team, 1929.

Boy Scouts in the 1930s.

Members of the Boys' Brigade in the 1930s.

GRIMSBY CITADEL BAND
BANDMASTER. W G FRIDAY

The Salvation Army band at the Cenotaph, Nuns Corner, 1933.

The Palace Theatre and Bar, Victoria Street, near Central Market, *c.* 1900.

The Regal Cinema, one of about a dozen in the town in the 1960s, opened in 1937 on the site of the old Prince of Wales Theatre in Freeman Street. It is pictured here in about 1960.

The Education Office cricket team, which included several staff from the Youth Employment Service, 1951.

The Education Office cricket team and head teachers, 1951.

The demolition of the Palace Theatre. The lady came down off the top first.

The Palace opened as a variety theatre in 1904 and was demolished in 1979.

Billiard players in 1943. The group includes H. Little (secretary, Grimsby Billiards League), Councillor Max Bloom (Mayor), R. Johnson, Sidney Lee, Jack Middleton, Joe Davis. Exhibition billiards were by Sidney Lee and Joe Davis, and Jack Middleton was probably the referee.